FLORAL

TRADITIONS

at the
Honolulu
Academy
of Arts

Text by
Kaui Philpotts

Photography by
Linny Morris Cunningham

Contents

Frontispiece: The gates at the main entrance are both beautiful and practical, allowing the trade winds to circulate freely.

Left: The floral displays inside the front entrance are the first "works of art" encountered by all visitors.

Director's Foreword

Visitors to the Honolulu Academy of Arts are impressed by the architecture and the collections, and by striking floral arrangements that are created on a weekly basis by a corps of loyal volunteers. These floral sculptures are a museum tradition, which began when the doors of the Academy were first opened in 1927.

Flowers in their tropical diversity, profusion, and variety are often used in forms and contexts that reflect the unique composition of Hawaii's population. Flowers represent aloha, and the museum's floral arrangements create a gracious ambiance that charms and makes welcome all our guests.

This publication documents and pays tribute to this tradition and the scores of people who have contributed their time and talent to enrich the Academy with brilliant bursts of form, line, and color, which often equal the paintings, sculpture, and other art forms displayed in its galleries. Indeed it is not uncommon for visitors to remark on the floral arrangements before commenting on the collections and building.

The artists who compose these "living sculptures" have made and continue to make a significant contribution to the quality of life that we enjoy in Hawaii. First guided by the energy and talent of Caroline Peterson and then by the drive and creativity of May Moir, these special individuals are owed our sincere appreciation and thanks. The work of Peterson and Moir has been documented in previous publications, but the overall floral arrangement program to which they have each made extraordinary contributions has never been singly treated, nor has Moir's contribution been adequately acknowledged. The inspiration for this volume came from Mary Philpotts McGrath, who lived across the street from May and often offered flowers from her garden for the arrangements at the Academy. She felt there should be a book about May's contributions to the Academy and spearheaded the committee that was ultimately formed to bring it to fruition. Sam Cooke, Claire Johnston, Evanita Midkiff, Alice Guild, Peggy Vollman, and I served with pleasure on this committee. The result of our collaboration is this tribute to May, an exceptional individual who is deservedly a legend in her own time. Undaunted by advancing age, she continues to serve as an example of much that we would hope to be and aspire to achieve.

Since the late seventies members of MOA Sangetsu have provided floral arrangements for our Japanese galleries where they complement the beauty of paintings and enhance the overall visitor experience. MOA arrangements add another dimension to floral displays at the Academy.

Support for this publication has been provided by Mrs. May Moir, Mrs. Muriel Flanders, Mr. and Mrs. Robert Midkiff, Mr. and Mrs. Douglas Philpotts, Mr. Donald Angus, and the Cooke Foundation. I am very thankful for their generous assistance.

Kaui Philpotts worked diligently and ably to research and write the text

Detail of Chinese stone horse
at the entrance to the Academy.

for this volume, and I am extremely grateful for her dedicated efforts on our behalf. Thanks are due to Bob Hirano, associate specialist at the Lyon Arboretum, and Heidi Bornhorst, garden columnist for the *Honolulu Advertiser,* for their help in identifying botanical names and to Alice Guild and Joanne Trotter for soliciting their assistance. A special note of thanks is also owed Tish O'Connor, who with great skill and creativity edited this volume; her writing and organizational skills were essential to the completion of this effort. Here at the Academy, Don Brown, who heads the museum's publications department, Anne Seaman, and Rhoda Hackler are owed our gratitude.

The elegant and beautiful photographs that grace this volume are the work of an especially talented artist, Linny Morris Cunningham. Linny spent hundreds of hours at the Academy capturing the beauty of the floral arrangements, architecture, and gardens. The superb quality of her work is readily apparent. As is always the case, Dana Levy of Perpetua Press, Los Angeles, has designed a distinguished publication, which bears witness to his special talent and creativity.

Finally I would like to thank the many floral artists who have given their time and shared their creativity to bring beauty into all our lives.

GEORGE R. ELLIS
Director

May Moir's sketch for a pu'olo *or traditional Hawaiian gift, indicates how it is constructed.*

Preface

by May Moir

THE FIRST TIME I walked through the back gate of the Honolulu Academy of Arts sometime in the late 1930s, I was carrying an armload of orchids for a show. During World War II the Academy orchid shows grew in popularity and attracted hordes of military personnel as well as kamaainas. I think I worked on every orchid show until they were finally discontinued after the war.

In 1950, I volunteered to work at the Academy. I was offered clerical work in the office, but because I had just retired from twenty-five years of doing much the same thing, I asked instead to assist Caroline Peterson in creating the weekly floral displays at the Academy. Peterson at the time was much sought after as a floral designer for private parties and businesses all over Honolulu. She had begun decorating the Academy shortly after it opened, using beautiful tropical flowers from the gardens of Cooke family members and their friends. Soon I began joining Peterson, her handyman George Kajihiro, and John Mochin Gaza, the Academy's longtime installation foreman, in putting up the large dramatic displays each week. I have always maintained my own garden, so I too added plant material to our creations.

In 1961 Kajihiro retired, making it more difficult for Peterson to do the weekly arrangements because she didn't drive. Her daughter-in-law, Dora Peterson, drove her whenever possible, and Gaza and I continued to assist her with the arrangements. In 1963 she retired, and I inherited her job.

That same year Kitty Thompson, who had designed the original Academy landscaping and stayed to supervise its maintenance, also retired. I offered to take on this additional task until they could find someone qualified for the position. Somehow twenty years went by before I finally turned the garden over to Sue Girton when my husband, Goodale, became ill.

As the Academy membership, staff, and events multiplied tremendously in the next few years and Gaza was needed for myriad different jobs, it became clear that I was going to need more help in creating the floral arrangements. Some members of the Outdoor Circle to whom I confided my need offered to give a hand. Three of these original volunteers are still part of the Monday morning team. Over the years volunteers have come and gone, but there has always been a large enough core group that four are in attendance each week.

The dedication of these volunteers alleviated the labor problem, but the plant materials available to us became more and more scarce as people gave up their large gardens. Our task becomes creatively more challenging as we learn to scavenge everywhere for anything that can be recycled. I sincerely hope that this wonderful tradition of using plant material donated from private sources will always be carried on at the Academy.

Over the years I have kept a weekly journal chronicling our floral creations. I have also written two books on floral sculpture and *The Garden Watcher*, a month-by-month guide to what is in bloom and how to use it. This book documents the floral tradition at the Academy, which we hope will inspire the reader.

The Academy

WHEN THE HONOLULU ACADEMY OF ARTS opened to the public in 1927, Mrs. Charles M. Cooke Sr., its founder and principal benefactor, saw her dream come true. Born in Hawaii of American missionary parents, she had acted in the belief that art was important to the lives of all the people of the Islands and that each person had a moral obligation to contribute to the community. She was dedicated to the principle that the arts lent distinction to life and at the same time provide man with a sense of his spiritual identity, both as an individual and as part of a historic process. Mrs. Cooke Sr. and her family had the means to fulfill their perceived responsibility to this ideal.

Anna Charlotte Rice was the youngest daughter of New England missionaries who had arrived in Hawaii in 1841. Born in Honolulu in 1853, she grew up on Kauai, in a home that was the center of cultural life and missionary activity. Her home in the Islands and her education at Punahou School and Mills Young Ladies Seminary in California nurtured her innate passion for beauty and her appreciation for all the cultures represented in Hawaii.

Anna Rice became the wife of Charles Montague Cooke, also the child of missionaries, on April 29, 1874. Eight years later Charles Cooke, by then a successful businessman and builder in Honolulu, moved his rapidly growing family into a large, three-story Victorian home on Beretania Street, then unpaved, out toward Waikiki. The trees of Thomas Square were still young and low allowing the Cookes a panoramic view, over "Old Plantation," the Ward family home, from Diamond Head to Honolulu Harbor.

In her new home Anna Cooke began her collection of art with what were known as "parlor pieces," displayed in the front room and collected by the Cookes in the art stores of Honolulu and on their more and more frequent travels to America, Europe, and finally Asia. For thirty years the Cooke's collection grew until the Beretania Street house was full to bursting, in spite of their having loaned many large objects to Punahou School, members of the family, and friends.

After Charles Cooke died in 1909, his family continued to live in the Beretania Street house, but as the years passed the children married and moved away. Finally Mrs. Cooke Sr. realized that she was living alone in an

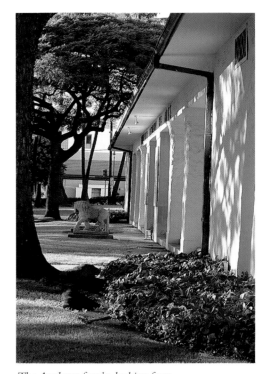

The Academy façade–looking from Victoria Street to Ward Avenue.

Opposite: Corridor off Central Court with a view of one of the niches in which weekly floral displays are placed.

aging mansion built of wood and filled with valuable art and antiques, that her children were worried about her safety in case of fire and, most important of all, she had not found a way to share her art collection with the local community. After a good deal of thought and numerous family consultations, she decided to tear down the old house, build a new home for herself on the hills above Makiki, and create an art academy on the Beretania Street property.

A local art scene began in the latter half of the nineteenth century when downtown storefronts displayed paintings or photographs by visiting artists for sale. The idea of an art museum for Honolulu became more formalized with the founding of the Kilohana Art League in 1897, to which Charles Cooke gave the use of a building at Beretania and Miller Streets for their cultural activities. In 1909 the Cooke family built an art gallery and addition to the library at Punahou School; in 1912 the family's collection of Old Master paintings was loaned to the gallery. The Kilohana Club, formerly the Kilohana Art League, was disbanded in 1913, but reborn as the Art Society in Honolulu by 1919. It is clear from all this activity that Honolulu was becoming more and more aware of art and anxious to participate in a variety of cultural activities. Mrs. Cooke, who by 1917 often opened her home to the public for exhibits by such artists as Lionel Walden and Charles W. Bartlett, was interested in assisting the burgeoning trend. Fur-

The Academy façade from Beretania Street.

Aerial view
of the Academy.

thermore, thanks to the Cooke Trust, she and her children were financially able to translate ideas into reality.

When Mrs. Cooke made up her mind to create a museum she turned to an old friend, Catharine Cox, a woman who was exceptionally well educated for the time, a teacher active in arts organizations in Honolulu, and a person in whose good judgment she had great confidence. Neither of them had any formal training in museum techniques, but they had a great fund of knowledge and a shining goal.

Rather than turning to one of the excellent local architects in Hawaii, Mrs. Cooke chose Bertram Grosvenor Goodhue, who came from New York to listen to the family members express their vision for the museum and to see other buildings in the Hawaiian tradition. She wanted a place that was restful and welcoming, where people would draw inspiration not only from the art displayed but from their surroundings. She was not disappointed with what Goodhue designed and approved of changes to the plan made by Hardie Philip after his partner's untimely death, especially the elimination of an "Oriental" tower. "You don't need a tower. The mountains provide it. You don't need color. That is provided by the bright blossoms of Hawaii's flowering trees and shrubs," he wrote. The simple plan seemed to sense the architectural potential of the gentle Hawaiian climate, with courts open to the sky and cooled by water trickling into fountains. The structure incorporated forms that the peoples migrating to this common soil, the Hawaiian

Islands, had brought with them. The old Polynesian-style pitched roof and a lanai reminiscent of those developed by the early missionaries spoke immediately of Hawaii and welcome, and the bold, simple forms of the stuccoed stone walls and heavy columns beneath the weathered tile roofs completed a sense of strength and timelessness.

Within the building the Chinese Court, surrounded by galleries full of the art of Asia, was placed to the west of the Center Court and the Spanish Court, the center of Western art, was located to the east. This orientation deliberately reconstructs Hawaii's location in the middle of the Pacific, with Asia to the West and Europe to the East.

The materials used in building the Acad-

LEFT: Central Courtyard with Emile-Antoine Bourdelle's La Grande Penelope. *The sculpture rests on a platform that is frequently used for outdoor performances.*

TOP RIGHT: Kinau Courtyard with Jacques Lipchitz's Mother and Child.

BOTTOM RIGHT: Metal grill work in Kinau Courtyard.

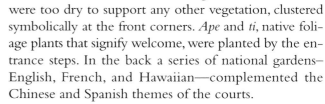

emy were carefully selected and reflected much of Hawaii's history. Granite slabs, quarried in China to serve as ballast in the ships that imported Hawaiian sandalwood during the early 1800s, were used as pavement; green-glazed tiles imported from China decorated the Chinese Court; Hawaiian lava rock was brought from Kaimuki; and an unusual aggregate stone in which shells were embedded was barged over from Molokai and cut into flagstones for the entrance and the inner courts.

In the edition of April 8, 1927, the *Honolulu Star Bulletin* called the building, "unassuming and a bit austere," but hailed it as "the first public building here in which a typical Hawaiian type of architecture has been evolved." The public came to form its own opinion: in the first month more than fifteen thousand people visited the new museum, an enormous turnout from a city that then had a population of just over 300,000.

The landscaping, designed by Catherine Richards Thompson, was as important to the whole concept of the Academy as was the structure. Using trees and shrubs with special significance to Hawaiians she created a strong and unified entrance to the building. Coconut palms frame the exterior, their swaying fronds pointing the way and their graceful shadows dancing on the lawn and the façade. Hardy hala *(pandanus)* trees, whose extensive root systems allowed them to survive on islands throughout the Pacific that were too dry to support any other vegetation, clustered symbolically at the front corners. *Ape* and *ti*, native foliage plants that signify welcome, were planted by the entrance steps. In the back a series of national gardens—English, French, and Hawaiian—complemented the Chinese and Spanish themes of the courts.

The finishing touch at the Academy has always been its magnificent flower arrangements, which embellish the lanais and galleries and are coordinated with the works of art. On opening day, when the people of Honolulu first entered the Academy of Arts, each gallery was filled with flowers arranged by Julia Giffard. The standard she set has been carried on and refined first by Caroline Peterson, with her assistant George Kajihiro, and then by May Moir and the loyal corps of volunteers who have formed around her. This book commemorates their tradition of excellence and artistry.

On April 8, 1927, when the dedicatory prayers were intoned, the songs sung, and the public was wel-

A water element is central to the plan of the Asian Courtyard. Aquatic plants are in bloom at all times.

*Roofline seen from the
Central Courtyard.*

A fanciful water course links brightly tiled fountains in the Mediterranean Courtyard.

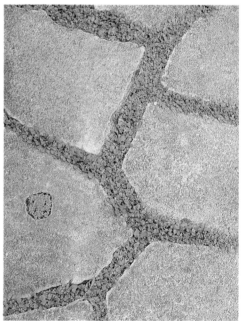

comed for the first time to the Honolulu Academy of Arts, Mrs. Cooke could be confident that she had achieved her goals:

> That our children of many nationalities and races, born far from the centres of Art, may receive an intimation of their own cultural legacy and wake to the ideals embodied in the art of their neighbors, that they may grasp that composite heritage accumulating for the new generations of Hawaii: That Hawaiians, Americans, Chinese, Japanese, Koreans, Filipinos, North Europeans, South Europeans and all other peoples living here, contacting through the channel of Art those deep intuitions common to all, may perceive a foundation on which a new culture, enriched by all the old strains, may be built in these islands.

Mrs. Cooke had opened doors not only to a building but to a whole universe and offered present and future generations of Hawaiians and visitors a knowledge of their inheritance and background, and a glimpse of the world's enduring beauty.

The physical plant has also been extended to meet increasing community needs and priorities. The Robert Allerton Library wing was constructed in 1956, followed by an education center in 1960. A cafe was opened in 1969 and the Clare Booth Luce wing, incorporating a large contemporary gallery, a 296-seat theater and administrative offices, was dedicated in 1977. Renovating the old Linekona School across Beretania Street, the Academy incorporated the Art Center in February, 1990 as an educational facility for the community, offering art classes for children and adults.

Mrs. Caroline Peterson

Caroline Peterson

Genius and Instinct

T O SAY THAT CAROLINE PETERSON SIMPLY HAD GOOD TASTE would not be telling the whole truth. She had a natural instinct for floral arranging that bordered on genius. For more than twenty-five years Caroline Peterson designed island-inspired arrangements for the Honolulu Academy of Arts that stunned, charmed, and provoked viewers to feel and see beyond ordinary beauty.

Nothing was too simple or too lowly that—if the texture was right or the color struck her just so — it wouldn't be considered for one of her often massive and always uncommon creations. Suddenly the peeled, reddish sheath of a banana stalk filled with sweet, yellow-centered plumerias looked harmoniously stylized. Cabbages or rhubarb came out of the kitchen and into an arrangement of rambling cottage roses. *Ti* leaves were tied into a basket filled with fragrant white gardenias.

"I love the rocks, the branches and stems, the trunks and stumps and the leaves, as well as the flowers," she once said. Peterson worked with what was around her. She loved bamboo, papyrus, and dried palm. A special favorite was the chartreuse color that the leaves of a young coconut branch brought to a design. Without formal training, she bent and manipulated nature at will.

"She is beyond flower arrangement. Mrs. Peterson approaches plant material like a sculptor approaches stone, or a painter his canvas. She is a true artist," wrote Kenneth Kingrey, an art professor at the University of Hawaii and Peterson's coauthor on *The Art of Flower Arrangement in Hawaii* (University of Hawaii Press, 1962), a book that used her designs and his text to explore a topic that was then largely unknown and establish it as a valid art discipline. He added, "We had to edit the photos of her work very carefully because some of them looked familiar. Everyone is now doing things she innovated forty years ago."

Her arrangements were "more than simply tasteful assemblages of interesting plant materials," said former Academy director Robert Griffing, Jr., "They are, instead, truly sculptural expressions so considered in their handling that they qualify as works of art." Calling Peterson's arrangements at the Academy the "most durably popular one-man show in the history of museums," Griffing theorized in his foreword to *The Art of Flower Arrangement in Hawaii* that if Peterson knew any so-called rules of floral design, "she

The gentle movement outward from a central core begins in the succulents (Aloe arborescens) at the heart of this monochrome arrangement, then changes abruptly to vigorous, upward-curving motion of the tentaclelike branches of another succulent (Graptopetalum paraguayense). The descriptions of Peterson's compositions are by Kenneth Kingrey from The Art of Flower Arrangement in Hawaii.

disregards—or deliberately breaks—them, depending solely upon her greatest asset, a sure aesthetic instinct."

May Moir, the designer who worked with her in the early 1960s and continues the tradition she began at the Academy, remembers Peterson as a quiet woman who was reticent in human interactions but reacted from her soul to everything in the plant world. "Creative minds are different. They see and feel something, and then the wheels get going." She rarely spoke about her work and taught by example, almost as if she couldn't explain why she did what she did, it was so natural to her. As her fame grew Peterson was often asked to do demonstrations, but Moir recalls that "she did not discuss what she was doing. I got a great deal from one demonstration at which Ken Kingrey discussed what she was doing and related it to design, which he taught at the University of Hawaii." Moir, who would later collaborate with Peterson in such demonstrations, acting not only as the assistant but verbalizing the process for the audience, understood "what a strain it is to keep up a patter while you are concentrating on the plant material and how the design is going."

Her daughter-in-law Dora Peterson describes her as a determined, independent person who understood her gift: "She never sacrificed her talent just to please someone." That talent may have been inborn—her daughter-in-law noted that "she had a natural longing for quality experiences and people," and sought "the kind of situations to learn and improve herself," overcoming great personal hardships with her will. Not until Peterson had married and raised her family of four did she have the time and the opportunity to reach out and explore her artistic gifts.

Caroline Wright was born in Koloa, Kauai in 1875, to an Hawaiian

This pu'olo or Hawaiian-style gift, demonstrates Mrs. Peterson's ability to combine such diverse tropical materials as ornamental bananas (Musa hybrid), heliconia (Heliconia bihai), ti leaves (Cordyline fruticosa), *and a white plumeria lei (Plumeria hybrid) into an arrangement reflecting the informality of Hawaii. A unifying element is the boat-shaped outline of the heliconia bracts, repeated in the fruit, the curved ti leaves, and the flower petals of the lei. (Description by Kenneth Kingrey.)*

mother and English father, who died when she was quite young. She was sent as a young girl to live with her father's relatives on a ranch in Santa Rosa, California. Her life on the ranch was filled with endless hard work and little opportunity for education. An uncle, who traveled regularly to the mainland, saw her unhappiness and arranged for her to return to Hawaii.

At age nineteen, she married Charles Frederick Peterson, a Yale-educated attorney in Honolulu, who, like her, had a Hawaiian mother; his father was Scandinavian. The Petersons raised their four children in a comfortable house on University Avenue at the entrance to Manoa Valley where Caroline tended a large garden that included a small, separate structure which served as her studio.

The death of her husband when their son Edwin was in his senior year at Yale was devastating to her. To pick up her spirits, the rest of the family insisted she attend Edwin's graduation in the spring. During a protracted

An antique bronze container, a moss-covered rock or two, and a few tightly curled leaves from the heart of a giant tree fern (Cibotium glaucum) create this arresting, almost surrealistic, composition that illustrates the dramatic potential of texture. The living animate quality of the fern fronds is heightened by the cold inanimate quality of rock and bronze; the silky golden wool that protects the unborn leaves contrasts sharply with the abrasive surface of the container. The moss on the rocks and the encrusted patina on the container act as transition between the two. The stark simplicity of unborn fern fronds rising cobra-like from rocks in a deliberately restricted container—much as the parent trees rose from a crevice in an old Hawaiian lava flow—retains the feeling of latent force, the embryonic about-to-burst-into-being quality of growing things. (Description by Kenneth Kingrey.)

visit to the east coast she visited gardens and spent three months doing window arrangements and giving floral design classes at Carbone's House of Flowers and Italian Pottery in Boston. Peterson was inspired by the exquisite pottery the firm imported, and her artistic sense exploded. Her window designs literally stopped traffic. She was becoming a plant sculptor.

Her professional career, which really began with that trip, grew to occupy the time once happily dedicated to her husband and raising her four children. Pansies and violets she raised in her Honolulu garden were so gloriously perfect that they were soon in great demand as gifts. Friends, and their friends, began calling her for special arrangements for weddings or parties. Everyone wanted something different, that didn't look like every other florist in town. With her fertile imagination Peterson delivered just what they wanted. "My search for new materials, or for novel uses of commonplace materials, is never ending. It seems to go on unconsciously wherever I am," she confided to one reporter.

She produced floral designs for Betty Farrington, Dagmar and Muriel Cooke, Alice Spalding, Wilhelmina Tenney, and Princess Kawananakoa, among the most prominent hostesses in Honolulu society of the day. Soon commercial jobs—designing the flowers aboard the Matson Navigation ships and the lobbies of the Bank of Hawaii—were added to her list of accomplishments. On special occasions she decorated Central Union Church.

When the Honolulu Academy of Arts opened in 1927, she began designing its floral displays twice a week, arriving before the museum opened to the public, to do her work. In these arrangements she developed the tradition of using the Hawaiian plant materials that were at hand to their highest artistic end. The environment at the Academy was one of the fertile situations that she had long craved: "I've learned so much here. The Academy is such a wonderful place to work," she said.

John Mochin Gaza, who worked for forty-six years (1926-1971) as installation foreman at the Academy and knew where everything was, understood Peterson and what she required almost without her asking. Peterson acknowledged Gaza as a collaborator. Pointing him out at work, helping assemble a large arrangement, she informed a journalist who had come to write about her work, "That's Gaza. He's an artist, too." Peterson also relied on her longtime assistant, George Kajihiro, who was also an artist in his own right, for help with the over-sized creations, as well as in maintaining her own garden.

The enigma of Caroline Peterson was that she was at once confident of her talents and privately very shy, a condition that may have stemmed from her difficult childhood. She never attended the grand parties she decorated, even though the hostesses loved her and invited her over and over again. What she enjoyed most was the creative process of designing innovative arrangements to complement sumptuous settings, using containers that were art objects in themselves.

By 1950, when Peterson was invited by the Garden Club of America to lecture and demonstrate in several mainland cities, she was recognized as a master of island floral design. Her arrangements were featured in *Vogue* and *House Beautiful* magazines, helping to popularize the creative potential of Hawaii's rich floral legacy. Caroline Peterson knew the leaves and the curve of every flower, branch, and vegetable. But as a native daughter of the islands, she was most inspired by what was inherently Hawaiian in origin. Her work and vision remain an inspiration today.

May Moir pauses for reflection during the creation of an arrangement.

May Moir

Talent and Tenacity

A LTHOUGH INITIALLY MAY MOIR'S route to her destiny was circuitous, it is difficult to imagine her not becoming the artist and designer she is today. The opportunites for women in the first decades of the twentieth century might have thwarted less passionate interests, but nothing could have kept this determined woman, who is always simply dressed in slacks, from doing something she wanted.

Born in 1907 as the only child of a Scottish mother and Norwegian father, May Arstad eagerly sought ways to interact with the world. Even as a toddler, her headstrong nature and tomboy aesthetic were evident: she drove her mother mad planting tree seeds in the flower beds of their Kaimuki garden, an early indication of what was to come. Her winning ways soon attracted a soulmate in the garden next door where "Grandma Hall," a New England expatriate, patiently nurtured the young child's love of gardening.

At Punahou School, always independent and curious, May showed more interest in drafting class than home economics. But in the 1920s girls took home economics as they were told. When she sought employment in 1926 as a Punahou graduate, she applied for a job assisting the layout artist at the *Honolulu Star-Bulletin,* but accepted instead a receptionist job that paid two dollars more a week.

In 1928 May married Charles M. Neal, a man as enthusiastic about plants as she. Together they gardened every inch of their hillside lot in Kailua, before it became the sprawling bedroom community of today. After their daughter Peggy was born in 1933, May left her bookkeeping job at Pacific Chemical. When Peggy went off to kindergarten, May began marketing her homemade preserves, creating a business that flourished until rationing was imposed during World War II. She also joined her husband in developing his real estate business, becoming licensed as a broker herself. When a heart attack prematurely killed Charles Neal, May worked in real estate and raised her young daughter.

With W. W. Goodale Moir, an agronomist with American Factors and chairman of the board of the Hawaii Sugar Planters Association, a mutual interest in plants became a shared passion that shaped their life together. Goodale and May married in 1949 and set up housekeeping at his house in Nuuanu Valley. Their home was called Lipolani, which means "tropical

A view of the Moir garden.

A portion of the courtyard of the Moir residence, showing the diversity and beauty of this remarkable garden.

heaven" in Hawaiian. With its high ceilings and thick masonry walls, the house has the coolness of a dark cellar in mid-summer. Both the landscaping and interior decoration were rather conventional, but May soon began to put her stamp on the place. A grass lawn was replaced with a walled garden that shielded the house from the street, and heavy draperies were removed from the tall windows at the end of the living room, opening it to the garden.

"I always said he married me because he needed a good yard boy," she says, laughing. The Moir garden, which has been visited and photographed by garden enthusiasts for decades, has evolved in sections—each with its own flavor. From the gate a stone pathway descends to a courtyard by the front door. In late summer dozens of bright purple fish-shaped flowers poke from the bromeliads, which had all been generated from seed, lining the walkway. This garden is a showcase for the diversity of bromeliads, with huge clumps of *aechmea, neoregelia, nidularium,* and *vriesea* interspersed with succulents. The many branches of a tacoma tree stretch in the front corner of the lot, supporting a diverse colony of staghorn and other tree ferns, with anthuriums and orchids encircling the trunk. Part of the surrounding wall is constructed of hollow tile blocks turned sideways to let the breezes flow into the garden, thus allowing the many epiphytic plants such as orchids to be aerated.

Mosses cover the lava stones that pave the flat garden at the rear of the house. A dense border of heliconias, bird of paradise, and gingers ensures that some floral material is always in bloom; a clump of blue ginger brightens the masses of tropical foliage, including shiny red-streaked *ti* leaves, dracaena, and native *laua'e* ferns; and gardenias scent the air.

The remnants of a once-extensive orchid collection occupy an enclosed space adjacent to the living room. After many years of fighting bugs that prey on orchids, May is content to raise only a dozen of the hardier varieties, and even these recently had to weather hurricane-force winds that nearly stripped off the roof. Goodale Moir was already a nationally known orchid specialist when the couple met, and together the two roamed the world hunting for orchids in diverse, exotic tropical locations from the jungles of Panama and the Dominican Republic to Jamaica, Costa Rica, Southeast Asia, Madagascar, and Australia. Vacations were planned around the sugar technology conferences he attended. May would research ahead of time the locations of rare species of plants, make the travel arrangements, and contact all the knowledgeable people who shared their interest in plants that they hoped to meet while there.

The seating alcove at the end of
the Moir living room is a favorite
spot for viewing the garden.

The multicolored flowers of
bromeliads blooming in May's garden.

Goodale brought many new orchid varieties to Hawaii and hybridized them. May found the giant yellow heliconia, *H. caribaea,* which has become a standard with tropical floral designers, when she wandered off a jungle path in the Dominican Republic while on a plant-finding trek in 1955. They had permits to bring species other than orchids back to Hawaii, just in case such an opportunity arose. "I wouldn't budge until someone came and got me a piece of the root," she remembers. The treasure was entrusted to the staff at Foster Gardens, who gave May a cutting as soon as it was established.

May offered some of the first flowers of *Heliconia caribaea* to Caroline Peterson, whom she had been assisting in creating floral arrangements at the Honolulu Academy of Arts on a regular basis since 1950. It was a generous gesture that elicited a warm response from the normally shy and reserved Mrs. Peterson. Peterson taught by example rather than words, a process that suited her nature. By working with her, May learned her technique, in the manner one acquires a master's skills in a traditional apprenticeship. May also investigated the Asian disciplines, studying Chinese flower painting and arranging and learning Ikenobo, the oldest school of Japanese flower styling, from a Buddhist priest.

When Peterson retired in 1963, May became the principal designer of the floral displays. Because John Mochin Gaza, the installation foreman at the Academy, had assumed other duties and wasn't able to spend as much time with the displays, May enlisted the help of several prominent Honolulu women to assist her, forming a loyal volunteer corps who enjoy mastering their mentor's craft as well as the spirit of camaraderie and purpose that they share. Their involvement allowed May to take on other duties, maintaining the Academy's landscaping and interior courtyards as well as supervising the grounds staff. These activities earned her the unofficial title of artist-in-residence at the Academy and praise from then-director James W. Foster: "She gives unrecorded hours of her time and talent. Because of her, visitors to the museum have a different kind of experience from the usual museum goer. Her plants and arrangements complement works of art and are often works of art in themselves."

When George Ellis became director in 1982, he turned to May to spearhead the restoration of the Academy's Asian Courtyard, a project funded by the Garden Club of Honolulu and an assignment she clearly relished. David Woolsey, the landscape architect she recommended, not only was a committed gardener as well as a designer but had a long-standing interest in Chinese garden design that was reflected in his library. His design, like the original plan for the Academy, incorporated traditional and symbolic mate-

rials: May located a cache of green ceramic tiles in the Academy's basement, which was almost sufficient to refurbish the balustrade in the Chinese court, and then secured a donation of similar tiles from Betty Ho, a dedicated member of the flower-arranging crew, to complete that design element.

The restoration included the replacement of thirty-year-old plumbing, which entailed digging up all the old pipes that supplied the large pool as well as the irrigation system. Slabs of Chinese granite, which had been imported to Honolulu as ballast on ships during the era of the sandalwood trade, were selected as paving for the courtyard. The Academy had a quantity of these slabs, which May had once used to landscape a difficult shady area under a huge monkeypod tree (*Samanea saman.*) When that installation had been ripped out to make way for the sculpture garden, May had insisted that the stone be preserved for later use. Over the years pieces had been used throughout the building and grounds, but finally enough was located to complete the paving.

In selecting plants for an enclosed courtyard, the landscaper must deal with the ambient light, which changes radically each season as the sun changes course. Sun-loving Chinese rice plant (*Chloranthus inconspicuus*), which initially formed the perimeter border, did not thrive and was replaced with something that could tolerate six months of shade. The hardy iris *(Neomarica caculea)* in various shades of purple, blue, and white that Moir chose are a lovely complement to the sandpaper vine *(Petrea volubilis)* that each spring

drapes the court with lavender flowers.

George Ellis seconded his predecessor's assessment of May, and then some. "It was clear from this experience that May's reputation as one of the Academy's greatest assets was well founded. She not only meets everyone's expectations but sets the standard that we all follow. May is our living treasure, as irreplacable as any other work of art."

The illness of her husband, who died in 1985, forced her to curtail some activities at the Academy and she even contemplated retiring from the flower-arranging squad. But the solace of practicing her craft and the friendly interaction with the volunteer corps sustained her through her mourning and rededicated her to the goal of gracing the Honolulu Academy of Arts with local plant materials that reflect the beauty of the islands and perpetuate the goals of the museum's founder.

The longevity of the volunteers' involvement is sustained by the appreciation they receive from everyone who sees the stunning new arrangements in the five-by-seven foot niches in the interior courtyard and at the entrance every week. But they readily admit that the process itself is fun, and that their shared dedication has become a bond of friendship. One volunteer remembers that being asked to join the flower squad was "a red letter day for me, the start of an exciting new venture in my life" that has included entering and judging national flower shows. Her sentiments are shared by all of May's "girls": "I feel deeply grateful to May not only for giving me the

opportunity to learn and grow under her expertise and guidance but also for the ensuing activities that have developed from it...There are so many people whose lives she has enriched through her teachings and many generosities, including mine."

May's home workshop in her basement is organized clutter. Several different kinds of cutting shears hang within reach of her work table. There are wire cutters and containers. Upstairs, in the rafters of her garage, lie neatly catalogued stacks of dried branches from coconut palms and other tropical trees her creative eye found fascinating or beautiful, waiting to be selected for an arrangement. An old greenhouse holds more dried material, which always comes in handy when fresh plants are scarce.

Outside in the garden she has nurtured for almost fifty years, May finds inspiration and more than the occasional bit of plant material to contribute. "May's greatest joy is growing enough plant material to be able to cut with a lavish hand for the beautification of the Honolulu Academy of Arts," wrote Cynthia Eyre in the introduction to Moir's 1977 handbook on flower arranging, a statement that has been proven true countless times.

May Moir is a rare artist whose creative spirit is prodded not by excess, but scarcity. She hates waste about as much as she hates nonsense. What defines her is character—the good, old-fashioned kind that doesn't give up when at first you don't get just what you want. Like her masterpieces of floral display, May Moir is an original.

The Floral Corps Volunteers

FEW WHO MARVEL at the Academy arrangements realize that there is no budget for any of it—plants or labor—and there never has been any. When the Academy opened its doors, flowers were brought in from the large, manicured yards of Honolulu's most prominent citizens, especially the Cooke family estates. In those prewar days, great gardens were tended by family-employed yardmen, and providing expansive florals was less of a chore or expense than it is today.

That the floral tradition continues to flourish at the Academy has for the past thirty years been due largely to the efforts of May Moir and a volunteer corps working on a regular basis. One prerequisite for joining the volunteer corps of floral arrangers is that you maintain your own garden or have access to plants, because the floral material, as well as the labor, is all donated. Week in and week out, these women also scour backyards, roadsides, and rely on the good nature of neighbors for free material for their arrangements. One week it might be outsized white bird of paradise from Maunalani Heights, or the next an unusual branch of cinnabar-colored pods from Nuuanu Valley. In spite of, or perhaps because of these demanding conditions, the arrangements are always fresh, inventive, and artistically stimulating.

Each Monday morning the volunteers arrive at the Academy by seven a.m. Arrangements are usually suggested by the plant material that is offered, which May ponders and sometimes supplements with donations from her own garden or other sources. An arrangement always begins with a sketch—done by Moir to an informal scale, often drawn on the back of an envelope or on scratch paper—based on the materials she knows she will have on hand. The sketches help in determining the amount of supplementary material needed and in refining the design of the piece. Because the Academy arrangements are often massive—made to fill niches five feet wide, seven feet high, and 16 inches deep—the physical act of composing them is a collaborative effort, and May's sketches communicate her intent to the volunteers on Monday morning.

Once on site the group works quickly, pulling around their cart filled with rocks for anchoring the large and sometimes unwieldy pieces. Creative vision must be coupled with a firm grasp of construction technique because the arrangements must be firmly anchored to hold all week. (Conditions in the open courtyards can include strong drafts, as well as wilting heat and hu-

Alison Manaut puts the finishing touches on one of the weekly floral arrangements.

Phyllis Guard and May Moir

OPPOSITE: *The beauties of torch ginger are gradually revealed during its blooming cycle.*

Top: *A large and diverse collection of containers is available to meet various practical and aesthetic demands.*

Bottom left: *The process begins with a sketch for the arrangement being sculpted and proceeds in orderly, cooperative fashion, with volunteer Alice Guild assisting May. Moir contemplates the finished piece (bottom right).*

midity, and visitors sometimes find it impossible not to explore the displays with their fingers.) While the group works, May supervises—giving advice and then standing back, hands on hips, assessing their mutual achievement.

The first women to join the volunteer corps signed on as apprentices, ready and willing to help and learn in an informal setting. Because individual schedules were sometimes in conflict, the availability of a large group of trained volunteers was needed to ensure enough workers on every Monday morning. Moir, therefore, periodically teaches classes and asks the best students to join the volunteer corps. The longevity of the volunteers' involvement is sustained by the appreciation they receive from everyone who sees the stunning new arrangements that are created each week. But they readily admit that the process itself is fun, and that their shared dedication has become a bond of friendship. Newcomers are always welcome: join the group that forms at the Academy's back gate very early on Monday mornings or send a note introducing yourself and your interests.

FLORAL DESIGN: A DEMONSTRATION

The photographs below demonstrate the process of putting together one of the large arrangements at the Academy. The text summarizes the principles on which the arranger draws, not to suggest that they consciously recite such rules, but to help reveal the philosophy underlying the process.

To succeed a composition must embody two equally important principles: good design and sound construction. Poor execution can ruin a fine design and limit the staying power of the arrangement. By the same token, a sound arrangement without a design plan can become nothing but a shapeless mass in a container.

Like sculpture, a similar artform, tropical arrangements are three-dimensional and must always be thought of as a whole. Color adds excitement; line and balance give an arrangement backbone and texture. Establishing dominance gives an arrangement character, variation creates vitality, and repetition makes it more compelling. The transition between elements reveals the complexity of a piece: an effective juxtaposition of colors or textures, or successful combinations in a large-scale composition, for instance. Opposing elements create tension, setting up a conflict and allowing the individual elements to show off.

Balance can be either symmetrical or asymmetrical—formal with identical sides or free form. Which one your arrangement will be must be determined before the first branch is inserted. Moir often says that the arrangement is only as good as that first placement.

Through the discipline of turning out huge floral displays week after week, the volunteers have mastered these design principles, often learning important lessons from their mistakes. There are some rules specific to floral design at the Academy—never obscure the portrait of Mrs. Cooke with a bouquet, for instance—but even these state general principles: in this case, determine the scale of the composition in relationship to its surroundings. The negative space, including the shadow, is as important as the positive space.

May Moir gives this succinct piece of advice to the would-be floral designer: "Scrounge! Train your eye. You only see what you're looking for, so to see the full potential of a plant or a piece of driftwood or a cluster of flowers, you must train yourself to look for it. Once you learn to see beauty in the commonplace, the whole world looks better."

MOA Sangetsu
Transforming the Spirit

ANOTHER GROUP OF WOMEN also arrive at the gates of the Academy every Monday morning. In their arms are fresh flowers, their shears, and most importantly their attitude and spirituality. They are members of the Church of World Messianity who have come to arrange flowers for the Japanese galleries, and by this process they are furthering spiritual goals, which include the creation of a better world.

MOA Sangetsu, a school of flower arranging that is a branch of the broader discipline of Japanese floral technique called ikebana, is dedicated to the philosophy that through beauty the human spirit is enriched and the world made more harmonious. The MOA (the acronym derives from initials of its founder, Mokichi Okada) philosophy builds upon simple floral arranging tasks to create a spiritual attitude. The way the arranger feels and the habits of respect that structure his creation enter the arrangement and are communicated to the public. The result, according to its practitioners, is two-thirds *kokoro*, or heart, and one-third technique.

The Church of World Messianity was founded in 1935 by Mokichi Okada, a man born in Tokyo in 1882, who overcame an impoverished background and delicate health to prosper in business. Through personal tragedy—the loss of his wife and baby in childbirth and the financial panic which swept Japan after the Great Kanto Earthquake of 1923–Okada gained a vision of a New Age on earth in which human misery would be replaced by peace, beauty, health, and prosperity. He believed that all discord was man-made, the result of actions that were not in agreement with nature. Beauty and the appreciation of nature, he said, could improve a person's mental and spiritual consciousness.

One tenet of the church he founded in 1935 is that the arts are able to transform the human spirit. He wrote: "Those who love beauty have deep appreciation of all the fine arts, are people indeed living in Paradise in spirit." To realize this belief, the MOA Foundation established the Hakone Museum of Art in June 1952 and the MOA Museum of Art at Atami in 1982, as well as their flower arranging school. Okada enunciated goals for these institutions that reflect the church's philosophy: "Japan's mission is to contribute to the welfare of the world through the medium of beauty. For this purpose,

A beautiful arrangement created for the Japanese galleries.

OPPOSITE: *An arrangement created by the MOA team accents the tokonoma in which a scroll by Shiko Munakata is hanging.*

I am constructing in the scenic areas of Atami and Hakone models of an earthly paradise, and within these grounds I will establish museums."

Members of the Church of World Messianity are encouraged to help as many people as possible in their daily lives through the creation of beauty. Exponents of the MOA Sangetsu school of floral design practice the craft of floral arrangement and share what they do with the community at large, contributing arrangements to places frequented by the public. They believe that seeing and appreciating flowers will elevate the individual and collective spirit and that life for all would be enriched. "Those who deeply love and appreciate flowers, their grace, their beauty, have hearts which truly must be equally as beautiful," wrote Okada.

MOA Sangetsu sponsors floral design classes in more than twenty countries around the world. In Honolulu, members of MOA Sangetsu provide free floral arrangements to the offices of the Governor and Lt. Governor, the Mayor, several hospitals and health centers, the police station, the Japanese Consulate, and the Honolulu Academy of Arts.

MOA Sangetsu's involvement with the Academy began in the late 1970s when for more than a year two of its members, Jeanette Suzuki and Mariko

A member of the MOA team, Bless Ebesugawa, holding flowers that will be used in the Japanese galleries. Behind her are good luck offerings left by visitors to an exhibition celebrating the Japanese New Year.

Takeda, visited the Academy every Tuesday to see and admire the new arrangements created by May Moir and her volunteers. They had first admired arrangements Moir had made for the wedding of a Japanese friend's daughter at the Church of World Messianity, and then began visiting the Academy regularly to see her creations. Suzuki and Takeda, wives of ministers at the Church of World Messianity, are teachers of floral design and followers of the teachings of Okada, but this was a rare opportunity to study the western aesthetic, which they appreciated.

At the request of Director Jim Foster, Moir had ocassionally designed arrangements for the Japanese galleries, as had volunteers Joanne Clarke and Violet Gaspar, but she did not have the time or resources to undertake this assignment on a regular basis. She asked Suzuki and Takeda if MOA Sangetsu would add the Academy to its roster of public institutions, and the group has faithfully installed arrangements in the Japanese galleries ever since.

"We have a mission to make other people happy and to go out into society," they say. Pointing out that the Japanese character for "flower" means "god has been transformed," they note that the arranger must therefore show reverence for the flowers themselves because they represent truth, beauty, and virtue. Seeing these qualities of flowers—which it is the arranger's goal to reveal—reminds man that he should take care not to deviate from the natural order of things.

Their craft combines human skill with nature's beauty to create something better. They select flowers that are in season and durable because each arrangement must remain fresh for a full week. Among their favorites are chrysanthemums, "pin cushion" protea, carnations, Star of Bethlehem, dendrobium orchids, and safflower. Only fresh, never artificial, materials are used. The arrangements are sparse because by using fewer flowers, they believe each one can be viewed more clearly and appreciated for its own value. Their master, Okada, believed that plant matter should be handled quickly: "If you handle the flowers or branches too long, you weaken their vitality."

MOA Sangetsu followers say there are no "ten easy lessons" to spiritual awareness through flowers. They instead suggest meditation before beginning work to show respect for their founder, and on completing an arrangement, they clean up methodically. This ritualized process permeates all that they do—from assembling materials to clean up. The beauty of their arrangements is a testament to their philosophy and a joy for visitors to the Japanese galleries.

Floral Traditions
at the
Honolulu Academy
of Arts

Plate descriptions by
Letitia Burns O'Connor

*Shadows falling across the lawn of
the Central Courtyard.*

Special Events

SPECIAL EVENTS at the Honolulu Academy of Arts—the opening of a new exhibition, a luncheon for the directors of other American museums or the annual holiday celebrations from Thanksgiving through the New Year—are the occasion for extraordinary displays.

Encounters with Paradise, an ambitious exhibition organized by The Academy in January, 1992 to highlight images of the islands made by artists during the last 150 years, was a very special event that invited a celebration of native Hawaiian culture and included a poi dinner to thank the donors on the night before the galleries opened. *Kahili,* traditional Hawaiian symbols of rank, which were carried by bearers on occasions of special importance, were planned for the front entrance. A *kahili* consists of a large cylinder, about eighteen inches in diameter, of floral material that is often topped with feather work and mounted on a pole that might be twenty feet high. Plumeria blossoms are frequently chosen for the floral material and the pole is often draped with green *ti* leaves, but because of the duration of this exhibition, dried *Dracaena draco* leaves and dry tree fern fronds were used for this *kahili* .

Under the portait of "Mother Cooke," there was an ample arrangement of tropical fruits—accented with the bright colors of calamandon or "Chinese orange" *(Citrus mitis),* and starfruit, along with breadfruit and calabash. An ilima lei, threaded through the composition suggested the natural bounty of the islands and the generosity of the Academy's original benefactor. Although the display was beautiful for the party, it proved unstable and so was reworked with more durable and dried materials—including a paper version of the ilima lei, fashioned by Moir.

A kahili created by Moir for the exhibition, Encounters with Paradise.

OPPOSITE: *A portrait of the Academy founder, Mrs. C. M. Cooke, by C. W. Bartlett located at the museum's Information and Admission Center. The low horizontal arrangement was created for the exhibition,* Encounters with Paradise.

Assessing the flowers that were in bloom at that season, Moir chose the traditional Hawaiian colors of yellow and red to dominate the scheme. The *Heliconea caribaea 'Gold'*, or giant yellow type, which she had located in 1953 in the Dominican Republic and introduced to the Hawaiian islands, was blooming in her garden, so she cut those as well as seven mature heads of *ti* leaves (*Cordyline terminalis*), a generous donation that she modestly asserts she "had been wanting to cut as they had grown too tall outside the patio." For the larger display pieces, six "parrot's beak" heliconia (*H. psittacorum*), three Indonesian ginger (*Tapeinochilos anansassae*), a few "snakes" (*Calathea crotalifera*), some bixa pods (*Bixa orellana*) for a touch of red, as well as the giant yellow heliconias were added to *laua'e* fern (*Phymatosorus scolopendria*), a native loved for its fragrance that was used as the base for the arrangements.

The same flowers with clusters of red berries (*Ardesia crenata*) and stems of bright orange tangerines were arranged in wooden calabashes for the dining tables, creating exactly the environment that the Academy wished to convey to its guests, "namely that they were special and appreciated," as Director George Ellis enthused, noting that Moir had, implausibly, "once again outdone herself."

A dinner for donors to Encounters With Paradise *featured a poi supper.*

Inspired by the glass objects in *America in Glass,* an exhibition organized by the Corning Museum and presented at the Academy, September–November, 1983, May Moir decided to use only glass containers for the arrangements. A pair of glass cylinders, which had originally been five-gallon bottles, were cut and buffed to use for the pair of arrangements at the entrance to the museum. The floral design, a spiral of "moon glow" sansevieria and hydrangeas—blue in one arrangement and pink on the other—that wound around a sturdy piece of banana stalk continued right to the foot of the container, visible through the glass. The large kenzan required to stablilize the massive arrangement was painted aqua to blend with the glass and glass pebbles filled the bottom of the container as further disguise for the mechanics of the piece.

When a meeting of the Association of American Art Museum Directors was scheduled for Honolulu in January, 1991, a luncheon at the Academy was planned.

A donation of several dozen *Heliconia revoluta,* a dainty, bright red, hang-down form of this tropical standard, was used in several large display arrangements. Its red bracts and yellow rattlesnake plant formed a bright counterpoint to a base of large, perforated monstera leaves and whole heads of bronze *ti* leaves. A few other stalks of heliconia, including the bicolored lobster claw (*H. caribaea x H. bihai cv. 'Jacquinii'*) were added to the pendent red type and yellow rattlesnakes on a dark base of *ti* plants and spider lily leaves for a very dramatic piece (opposite).

Breadfruit *(Artocarpus communis),* starfruit *(Averrhoa carambola),* and tangerines were combined with the large, white flower of the monstera vine *(Monstera deliciosa)* and sprigs of red *Brassaia actinophylla* to make arrangements for the punch tables (above).

Imposed requirements can be stimulating or they can restrict the designer's response to the circumstances. Moir had little advance information about the size or coloration of the paintings that would occupy the niches that usually held flower arrangements during the exhibition *Chihuly Courtyards* (October, 1992), but she learned that the artist preferred arrangements in the Japanese style and so created low horizontal pieces, which were appropriate for the paintings as well as the space.

May Moir's priorities are creating and maintaining the weekly arrangements at the Honolulu Academy of Arts (she usually goes by on Fridays to ensure that the plant materials will look fresh all weekend) and working in her own garden, so she has never been active in the Honolulu Garden Club. It was therefore a particular honor to be invited to design a large piece for *Art Flora*, an exhibition of floral designs sponsored by the Garden Club and held at the Academy in April 1984. The location she was assigned, by the large window in the Luce Gallery, was prominent and visible from all sides.

Moir chose heliconia as the centerpiece of her composition because of their splashy colors, dramatic, primitive shapes, and their long-lasting qualities. The bright red flowers, rimmed with yellow, of the *Heliconia rostrata* cascade in a hang-down formation from three dozen tall stalks in this spectacular large piece. Although it loses some of its vibrant coloration a few days after cutting, *Heliconia rostrata* is one of the few heliconia that dries well and whose size and origins are compatible with the composition she envisioned. Large brown sheaths of Royal Palm *(Roystanca requia)* frame the eight-foot-high cluster of cascading heliconia and smaller pieces conceal the container.

Holidays

Moir begins planning the decorations for the November/December holiday season in September and submits her plans early to the maintenance staff. A full day, when the Academy is closed, is required to complete the installation in December, but months of preparation precede that busy day. Thanksgiving provides the opportunity to make unusual combinations of fruits and vegetables, often with more traditional flowers. A straw-colored winnowing basket overflowing with Indian corn, fruit, and nuts makes a welcoming display. *Ti* leaves, ranged upright along the back of the basket, elevate its profile and flower spikes of the bromeliad *Achmea mulfordii* rupture its silhouette; each also adds a contrasting color, enriching the complex composition. A bright mound of fruit overflows a wooden bowl in another inviting display.

Periodically, May Moir has agreed to teach a course on flower arranging, with the enrollment fee dedicated to the Academy's never-sufficient fund for materials. A course on Christmas decorations included priceless tips on how to use free materials commonly found in home gardens to make spectacular wreaths like those found annually at the Academy. These time-honored combinations are popular: Overlapping layers of shiny magnolia leaves (*Magnolia grandiflora*), festooned with dried Christmas berries (*Schinus terebinthifolius*) (stripped of leaves, which wilt) and tiny pine cones; three-inch sprigs of mock orange leaves, all laid in the same direction on a ribbon-wrapped base, with small straw-colored ornaments or tiny red bows.

One of the most dramatic wreathes is time-consuming to assemble, but its dried materials will easily last for several years. The fibrous material of coconut fronds covers the base; pointed pods from the African tulip tree, pinned to the back, add a starlike projection around the rim. Clusters of *ohia lehua* (*Metrosideros polymorpha*) and nuts from the sweet gum tree mounded on the front create such a rich, textured surface that even a ribbon is superfluous.

Many people are surprised to discover that Spanish moss, called *hinahina* in Hawaii, is a bromeliad *(Tillandsia usneoides)*. One year Moir draped the moss on forms covered in green ribbon, then added air plant leaves, lipstick pods, and a bow with streamers for stunningly original wreathes.

Inspired by ancient Hawaiian capes and ceremonial cloaks made of bird feathers, Moir devised a similar scheme for the Academy's Christmas decor using turkey feathers. When dry, *Protea neriifolia* looks like feathers and was effectively combined with fresh greens and gilded pods of looking-glass tree (keel nuts), *Heritiera littoralis*, which are native from east Africa eastward to islands of the Pacific.

Moir claims to be a traditionalist, because she prefers the holiday colors of red and green, gold and silver, but she is never inhibited in her choice of unusual plant materials and imaginative combinations. This is the season of blissful excess, which is reflected in the big and strong treatments that have the impact she favors. In one memorable piece, which rose nearly five feet from a temple water bowl, hands of green Bluefield bananas were surmounted by a pyramid of flaming red flowers of *Musa coccinae*. These beautiful banana flowers are very long lasting, staying fresh for a month.

BOTTOM

The "Christmas heliconia" *(Heliconia braziliensis)* has red bracts and white flowers. Its short blooming season coincides with the holiday period, and it will keep for a week or more when arranged.

OPPOSITE

One standby is red blooms, which say "holiday" with a bang. Red anthuriums arranged in a low rectangular, metal container with stems of red coffee berries use traditional Christmas colors in an original, decorative piece. The frayed silhouette of curly willow breaks the perfect symmetry of the anthurium flowers.

Vertical garlands flanking the Academy entrance are a constant element of the holiday decor, but the design changes each year. Traditional greens, in this case, Norfolk Island pine, the rich browns of pine cones and pods of the looking-glass tree, and red infloresences of two bromeliads make a fresh and festive garland. Gilded leaves of *Sterculia apetala* form a bright base for the holiday swag at right, combined with tips of Norfolk Island pine and a variety of bromeliads—clusters of plump lavender berries from *Portea Petropolitana* and apple-green infloresences of *Tillandsia cyanea*.

OPPOSITE

At the New Year, the Japanese tradition of erecting *kadomatsu*, or "gate pines," arrangements featuring fresh pine branches that flank the entrance gate of residences and the door to shops throughout Japan, is practiced at the Academy. The time-honored arrangement includes bamboo, which symbolizes longevity, and pine, a symbol of seasonal regeneration, lashed together in a classic manner and mounted on a straw-covered base with split wood, which is considered a talisman against ill fortune.

This *kadomatsu* was arranged by Fujio Kaneko, the installation designer at the Academy, who can always be counted on to help the Floral Corps volunteers resolve technical problems. When the traditional needle pine is unavailable, Norfolk Island pine is substituted in its place.

Weekly Arrangements

Each of the plants combined in this piece is independently a strong element, a condition that could lead to visual cacophony unless controlled by good design, as here. The rich coloration and rounded form of the spider lily bulblets *(Crinum asiaticum)* contrast with the surrounding long waxy green leaves. The red of the lobster claw heliconia *(H. bihai)* echoes the bright flower of the *Neoregelia compacta*.

OPPOSITE
The vivid coloration of rainbow heliconia *(H. wagneriana)*, which has greenish-yellow bracts with rouged cheeks, as well as its large size and the dramatic articulation of its form suggest a simple composition when used in mass, as here. Five flowerheads, each more than a foot in height, create strong diagonal lines, alternating right and left in a form that mirrors that of the heliconia itself. The long, striped leaves of the hala or screw pine *(Pandanus potectorius)*, a tree native to Hawaii, will hold their shape when folded, conterbalancing the vertical thrust of the arrangement with a downward line. This large rainbow heliconia begins its blooming season in March and lasts through May, so it is a harbinger of spring in Hawaii.

Seasons in tropical climates have a way of gently slipping one into the other so subtly as to be barely noticed. But seasons they are. The transition within this piece—from torch ginger (*Etlingera elator*) closed at top to fully open at bottom—suggests the evolution of spring. In terms of the principles of flower arranging, this arrangement illustrates how repetition can be made dynamic by the use of progression, the slight variation within repeated elements that establishes rhythm. When unopened, waxy pink petals are folded in a torchlike formation around the large flower head, which often reaches eight inches in diameter. The overlapping petals of the interior suggest a very tropical rendition of a pinecone, which is gradually revealed as the exterior petals fold down. The dark purplish sheen of Queen Emma spider lily (*Crinum augustum*) leaves is a quiet foil for the florid torch ginger. The horizontal line of the shallow, open bowl, weighted with rocks, balances the strong vertical thrust of the flowers.

OPPOSITE

The dominant elements of this analagous color scheme—bright lavender-pink bracts of the flowering banana *(Musa rosea)* with the rich purplish mahogany of spider lily bulblets—create a luscious spring arrangement. Ornamental bananas (*Musa spp.*) will endure for a month after cutting, and the vividly colored bracts will unfurl successively, revealing fresh yellow flowers enclosed within and adding the dimension of transition to a floral arrangement. The agitated silhouette of the piece is created by the dynamic diagonal lines of the banana flowers and the jagged outline of "rickrack" Epiphyllum (*Epiphyllum ssp.*), as well as the row of small green bananas (*Musa acuminata*) lining the front rim of the bowl.

A few trimmed areca palm leaves
(*Chrysalidocarpus lutescens*) add a diagonal line
to a piece dominated by the large vertical
flowerheads of bright red lobster claw
heliconias *(H. bihai)* . The large purplish leaf of
ti negra Cordaline (*Cordyline fruticosa 'Negra'*) and
feathery Moa fern *(Psilotum nudum)* anchor the
soaring composition in a footed metal bowl.

OPPOSITE
The large, erect red heliconias *(H. caribaea
purpurea)* need only a subtle complement in this
tall arrangement. The silvery stalks of the
heliconia form a natural contrast with the dark
cycad fronds (*Cycas revoluta*.) The saturated
scarlet and large size of the inflorescences are so
dramatic that Moir arranges them simply,
allowing them to offer a regal, tropical greeting
to visitors to the Academy.

Cutting stems down to just the large flower head of such species as the white bird of paradise, Tahitian red ginger, and types of heliconia, can make for an interesting change in perspective and scale. May Moir cautions her apprentices that they mustn't think that because a flower came with a long stem it must stay that way. In this piece giant yellow heliconia stalks, which will last three weeks in water, are recycled, cut down and combined with lacy circles of coral in a shallow, wide bowl.

OPPOSITE

Like the golden light of autumn, an opulent grouping of giant yellow heliconia forms a glowing center in this tall arrangement. The trimmed fronds of the Areca palm give an erect form to this piece standing sentinel at the entrance to the Academy.

This simple arrangement could have been created in either spring or fall as this plant has at least two bloomings per year: in May and off and on through the fall. The yellow caribaea has special meaning for May Moir, because it was she who saw it for the first time in 1953 on an orchid-collecting trip in the Dominican Republic and was successful in introducing it to Hawaii. After spending two months in quarantine, the plants were nursed along by Foster Gardens personnel.

Ferns make a welcoming, bright arrangement in months when flowers are scarce. The repetition of colors is a compelling element in this monochromatic design, although the spore side of the tall bird's nest fern *(Asplenium nidus)* is revealed for a touch of contrasting brown. The contorted ends of curly tip fern *(Polypodium polycarpum grandiceps, cristolum)* expands the line and the feathery tendrils of leather fern *(Psilotum nudum)* or Moa, which means "chicken" in Hawaiian, forms a gentle base for the composition.

Opposite

A clever and pleasing composition combining horizontal and vertical lines is built around the perpendicular juxtaposition of the bracts of deep yellow *Heliconia latispatha* and tall leaves of the ladovia palm, whose verticality is echoed in their pleated texture. Clumps of bedding bromeliads and bulblets of the spider lily *(Crinum asiaticum)*—a plant easily raised in the home garden that May Moir finds indispensable for its leaves and the seedlike stage featured here, more than for the lovely flower that will only endure for a day—anchor the soaring composition.

The niches in which two large arrangements are usually placed have painted blue backgrounds which were part of the Christmas decor, transforming the space surrounding these compositions. The subtle coloration and warm tones of these pieces are given added definition by the cool background color. The arrangements feature dried materials—the pleated leaves of the fan palm *(Livistona chinensis)* add texture and establish a tripartite rhythm within the space. At left, the dried inflorescence of *Kalenchoi beharensis* cascades down the sinuous form, and the soft velvet leaves of the same plant and rich purple leaves of *Rhoeo discolor* brighten the base. Dried red flowers serve the same function in the matching piece at right.

Opposite
Bright colors, which tend to advance into space, can be used to add movement to a composition, as the stalks of lobster claw heliconia (*H. bihai* '*Lobster-claw*') do in this setting of dried fan palm and sansevieria.

These three totally different arrangements are based on the same plant material, orangey-red Java olive *(Sterculia foetida)* pods. The soaring thrust of three fringed cycad fronds and the bright red centers of *Neoregelia compacta* balance the color dominance of the pods in the original composition (opposite). The contrasting textures of the three plants used in this piece emphasize the scale and balance of the compostion. In a later, smaller piece (top), a branch of the same pods, now split open, is set upside down in an unusual composition that is softened only by the surface quality of the added velvet leaves of *Kalanchoe beharensis*. In its third manifestation (bottom), a tabletop piece in a red lacquer bowl, the split spheres of the smooth, glossy sterculia pods are combined with prickly pods of lipstick plant *(Bixa orellana)*, the rounded forms of the yellow pomelo and orange calamondin, and the irregular shapes of velvet leaf.

"Nature didn't make pairs," May Moir states tartly, noting that the two niches in the courtyards are separate, and so elaborate efforts to make the two large pieces identical would probably go unnoticed. In the arrangement opposite, dried materials—Royal palm sheathes, sugar cane, orange-rimmed bracts of *Dracaena draco*—are combined with fresh green succulents—long strips of epiphylum and flowerlike clusters of jade plant. Molokai sugar cane (*Saccharum officinarum*), a very decorative variety with dark purple-red stalks, is no longer removed from that habitat to restrict the spreading of smut, a cane disease, but a few pieces of the Molokai cane that were transplanted years ago in the volunteers' gardens are now a good source for cuttings.

In the simple arrangement at right, the freshness of the palm sheathes is shown by revealing the inside, still bright white, as well as the golden brown exteriors. Tall spikes of sansevieria and golden bromeliad flower complete the composition.

The striking coloration of this bromeliad flower, *Aechmea ramosa*, draws attention to its form. Knotted leaves of the hala tree (*Pandanus tectorius*) add variation to the lines of the piece, arranged simply in a celadon vase made by local ceramist Jerry Meek. The hala or screw pine, a tree native to Hawaii, has leaves up to four feet long that may be plaited into hats, baskets, and mats or just twisted for decorative effect, as here, where they add bulk to an arrangement.

OPPOSITE
An analogous color scheme, from orange to purple on the color wheel, features the bushy two-foot-long flower stems of the bromeliad *Portia petropolitania* combined with large Calathea leaves (*Calathea spp.*) and small red *ti* leaves. The many colorful varieties of the *ti* plant (*Cordyline terminalis*), a rosetted shrub that is a member of the lily family, appear first on May Moir's list of plants that are a must for the flower arranger. There are many variants in the pink and red range, as well as red-margined and round-leaf types; whole heads of the many dwarf varieties can be used to form a bouquet or as a strong element in a large composition. Moir cites two types as collector's prizes: 'Peter Buck' has a wide leaf in shades of apricot and rose; and *ti negra* (*Cordyline fruticosa 'Negra'*) has a very long, and long-lasting, dark purple and green leaf that appears almost black in color and so forms a strong background for bright flowers. The early Hawaiians used a row of the plants as boundary markers, in recognition of their tenacity once established, and tradition holds that a *ti* plant at the right of a home's entrance wards off evil spirits.

Both the form—a pendent variety with a snaky axis— and the florid coloration of the "sexy pink" heliconia *(H. chartacea)* suggest an austere arrangement: here, stripped stalks rise on a strict vertical axis from a glazed ginger jar without any added foliage. Spotlighting not only accents the intensity of this flower's coloration but creates fascinating shadows that exaggerate further its unusual form. Each vivid pink bract is rimmed with stripes of white and apple green and disguises multiple florets, which emerge as the bract matures, forming a soft fringe. This variety of heliconia blooms off and on throughout the year and, when cut, can last up to two weeks in an arrangement.

OPPOSITE

Fuzzy orange hanging heliconia *(H. mutisiana)* is a rare specimen, introduced to Hawaii in the last decade from its native Colombia. A fellow gardener, Leland Miyano, presented his first foot-long flower head to May Moir who arranged it with spider lily leaves in a dark-glazed pot. A cluster of immature spider lily bulblets and leaves resting on a lacquer plaque adds another element to the arrangement.

Many people would be delighted to receive a dozen red, flat, perfectly matched anthuriums as a gift, but not May Moir whose tastes run more to the voluptuous creations of nature, complete with its mistakes and flaws. Asked how she would solve the problem of the uninspired anthuriums, her creative mind starts churning, drawing on years of construction know-how. First add something to break up those "big, red hearts," she says, perhaps dark red *ti* leaves to give them more interest, then cut their long stems to different lengths and secure them in the vase to give the arrangement variation in height. The specimens in this arrangement, somewhat more irregular in color and form than our hypothetical example, are arranged with very slender branches of a dried palm infloresence to soften the effect.

OPPOSITE

The selection of a container, the first step in floral construction, should not be restricted to conventional vases. Most objects, such as a wooden or lacquer bowl, can be made to accommodate water and a flower holder without being destroyed. May Moir cautions novices to bypass complicated shapes, as well as elaborately decorated ones, in favor of simplicity. She prefers metal, wood, or ceramic in earth tones for tropical flowers. In the arrangement opposite, the textured surface of an earthenware bowl mirrors the ridged scallops of waxy plant material in the eight-inch flowerheads of golden beehive ginger *(Zingiber spectabile)*. The red edges of the *ti* leaves echo the coloration of the ginger; flowering spikes of the bromeliad *Aechmea ramosa* and rattlesnake ginger *(Calathea crotalifera)* add height to the composition.

Summer is the season to be fearless in combining colors. One daring arrangement (top) that graced the Academy one Labor Day weekend mixes vanda orchids *(Vandopsis lissochiloides),* which are magenta on the back side and spotted yellow on the front, with *ti negra* and a head of miniature *ti* leaves. The squat form of a green-glazed ginger jar and the mass of dark foliage form a solid base for the exuberant diagonal of the flamboyant flowers.

OPPOSITE
Gingers are particularly abundant in the summer season: white and yellow *(Hedychium coronarium* and *H. flavescens),* kahili *(H. gardnerianum),* Indonesian *(Tapeinochilos ananassae)* and shell *(Alpinia zerumbet)* are all available. Bright spikes of showy red ginger *(Alpinia purpurata)* are combined with a few nodding heads of white shell ginger, which is called in Hawaiian *awapuhi-luheluhe,* or "drooping ginger," and its large variegated leaves in a loose and exuberant composition.

BOTTOM
A low bowl brimming with sugar cane, *ti* leaves, and huge flower heads of red ginger seems at first glance to be a native Hawaiian ensemble. Although red gingers *(Alpinia purpurata)* are native to the western Pacific, they were purposefully introduced to Hawaii, where they have flourished. Called Tahitian ginger in recognition of its origin, these huge blooms are a double-flowered form: from within each bract on the flower spike a flowerlet emerges and continues to grow, until the tight cone has become a shaggy, heavy head, as here.

Cut down to just the rigid winged bracts, the heavy inflorescence of the Traveler's tree *(Ravenala madagascariensis)* is an exotic element that dominates this stark composition. Some claim that this native of Madagascar got its name from a tendency to orient itself under natural conditions on a north-south axis, acting thus as a compass for travelers; others assert that travelers gravitated toward it to drink the large amount of water that collects between its stems. In Madagascar entire hillsides may be covered with "Ravana," the local name, and its dried leaves are a common material for thatching.

Coconuts help to weight the heavy bract of Traveler's tree in a smoke-glazed low bowl of irregular shape. Like the white bird of paradise *(Strelitzia nicolai),* to which it is related, the infloresence consists of very large bracts that sprout from the leaf axil of the huge fanlike tree. Its seeds, which emerge later, are a fuzzy peacock blue, adding a startling contrast in colors.

OPPOSITE

On a lean Monday morning, the crew improvised with dried material: a five-foot palm inflorescence, dried, is combined with *Neoregelia compacta,* which creates a striking piece. Asymmetric balance is achieved by melding two contrasting halves in this dramatic composition: the mottled greens of sansevieria and waxy florets of bromeliads are mounted into a strong vertical line that complements and highlights the rough, stringy and linear texture of the palm. Sansevieria adds a strong line and height to the arrangement. This plant is especially useful when flowers are scarce, and it can be arranged without water.

ABOVE LEFT
Bird of paradise, *Heliconia psittacorum,* and satin pads of platycerium (*Platycerium spp.*) are combined with dried material and the bromeliad *Aechmea ramosa* in this casual arrangement placed in a split bamboo basket.

ABOVE RIGHT
Inflorescences of *Aechmea caudata* arranged in a row between two groups of dark *ti* leaves create a strong diagonal line in this piece. The contrasting textures of these two plant materials heighten the impact. The strong dark color of *Neoregelia* 'Fireball' at the base contrasts with the otherwise analogous color scheme—from orange-yellow though maroon—that extends even to the brass container.

OPPOSITE
A successful composition often has a dominant linear movement: three dried stalks of bamboo, cut to different heights, establish a strong vertical axis in this piece. A shot of yellow spray paint, rubbed off, brightens dried bamboo, which can be a dull putty color without enhancement. Combined with bright orange-red spikes of bromeliad flowers and a base of light green bedding bromeliads, which can be replanted when the piece is disassembled, this sumptuous piece showcases the traditional colors of autumn, when these bromeliads are in flower.

Volunteers

First Volunteers *(formed 1965)*

Joanne Trotter *(still active)*

Phyllis Guard *(still active)*

Ellin Burkland

Currently Active

Kitty Dillingham Budge *(from 1965)*

Alison Manaut *(from 1975)*

Betty Ho *(from 1977)*

Sally Moore *(from 1981)*

Alice Guild *(from 1990)*

Pauahi Clark *(from 1993)*

Emeritus Members

Yvonne Armitage

Joanne Clark

Judy Dawson

Bonnie Eyre

Stephen Haus

June Humme

Molly Nurse

Jean Stemmerman

Christmas Crew

Sue Girton

Lyn Lalakea

Jeannie Marchant

Margo Morgan

Tita Stack

ISBN: 0-937426-31-8

Copyright © 1995 by the Honolulu Academy of Arts.

All rights reserved.

Additional photography:

Werner Stoy: pp. 22, 24, 25, 26

Raymond Sato: p. 28

Tibor Franyo: pp. 47, 48, 49, 51, 52, 53, 55, 57, 58, 59, 66, 86

Floral Traditions at the Honolulu Academy of Arts

was produced by Perpetua Press, Los Angeles.

Edited by Letitia Burns O'Connor

Designed by Dana Levy

with the assistance of Darlene Hamilton

Typeset in Bembo on a Power Macintosh

Printed by South Sea International, Hong Kong.